American Biographies

SITTING BULL

Ann Weil

Chicago, Illinois

www.capstonepub.com
Visit our website to find out
more information about
Heinemann-Raintree books.

To order:
☎ Phone 888-454-2279
💻 Visit www.capstonepub.com
to browse our catalog and order online.

© 2013 Heinemann Library
an imprint of Capstone Global Library, LLC
Chicago, Illinois

Edited by Abby Colich, Megan Cotugno, and Laura
Hensley
Designed by Cynthia Della-Rovere
Original illustrations © Capstone Global Library
  Limited 2011
Illustrated by Oxford Designers & Illustrators
Picture research by Tracy Cummins
Originated by Capstone Global Library Limited
Printed and bound in China by Leo Paper Group

16 15 14 13 12
10 9 8 7 6 5 4 3 2 1

Library of Congress Cataloging-in-Publication Data
Weil, Ann.
  Sitting Bull / Ann Weil.
    p. cm.—(American biographies)
  Includes bibliographical references and index.
  ISBN 978-1-4329-6449-8 (hb)—ISBN 978-1-4329-
6460-3 (pb) 1. Sitting Bull, 1831-1890. 2. Dakota
Indians—Kings and rulers—Biography. 3. Dakota
Indians—Wars. I. Title.
  E99.D1S627223 2012
  978.004'9752—dc23   2011037573
  [B]

Acknowledgments
The author and publishers are grateful to the
following for permission to reproduce copyright
material: Corbis: pp. 7 (© CORBIS), 15 (© CORBIS),
23 (© Nik Wheeler), 40 (© Arno Burgi/dpa), 41 (©
Connie Ricca); Getty Images: pp. 9 (Buyenlarge), 31
(MPI); Library and Archives Canada: p. 33 (© Public
Domain Source: RCMP); Library of Congress Prints
and Photographs: pp. 5, 6, 16, 19, 21, 25, 29, 34, 35,
39; Nativestock.com: pp. 11 (© Marilyn Angel Wynn),
12 (© Marilyn Angel Wynn), 13 (© Marilyn Angel
Wynn); Shutterstock: pp. 10 (© Jim Parkin), 17 (©
Don Bendickson), 22 (© Jill Battaglia), 37 (© Martha
Marks); The Granger Collection: pp. 27, 28, 36.

Cover photograph of Sitting Bull by D.F. Barry, 1885,
reproduced with permission from Getty Images
(SuperStock).

Contents

Some words are shown in bold, **like this**.
These words are explained in the glossary.

A Legend

A people without history is like wind on the buffalo grass.
    —Lakota saying

Around 1831 a boy was born on the banks of what his people called the Elk River. Today people call it the Grand River. The place where he was born is now part of South Dakota. But at the time of his birth, the United States was still forming. This baby boy was born to a **band** of American Indians called the Hunkpapa. The baby's father, Returns Again, gave his infant son the name Jumping Badger. The boy would have several names during his lifetime. We remember him as Sitting Bull.

History and culture

Sitting Bull is a legendary figure. And when a person becomes a legend, facts and opinions jumble together. Over the years, it becomes harder to find the truth in the stories, especially when the stories belong to two very different **cultures**.

Almost all written history of Sitting Bull's life comes from white Americans who did not understand his language or his religion. They did not appreciate the relationship that had developed between his people and the land they had been taking care of for generations.

American Indian history was not written down. It was retold to each new generation. This knowledge was not available to outsiders until recently. Now American Indians are sharing their stories with the world. Sitting Bull's great-grandson put his family's stories into a book and two DVDs that give all Americans a better understanding of how this great man shaped their country and what it means to be an American.

Sitting Bull sat for many portraits after he surrendered in 1881. In this one he is holding a peace pipe.

The Lakota

The Hunkpapa are part of the Lakota Nation. The Lakota, a part of the Great Sioux Nation, were a North American Indian superpower in the 1830s. And Jumping Badger was born into one of the Lakota's most powerful and respected families.

Lakota babies were strapped to **cradleboards** and carried on their mother's back.

This photo shows Sitting Bull's camp in the 1870s.

At the time, the Hunkpapa were **nomads**. They hunted bison, or buffalo. When the great buffalo herds moved, the Lakota packed up their homes and belongings and followed them. Jumping Badger traveled in a cradleboard strapped to his mother's back or attached to a horse. His family's home was a **tipi**. This was a cone-shaped structure made of wooden poles and buffalo **hides**. It was taken apart and pulled behind horses each time the **tribe** moved.

From "Jumping Badger" to "Slow"

It was common for a boy's name to change as he grew and showed different parts of his personality. The infant named Jumping Badger grew into a boy who was called Slow. Slow can mean weak or stupid. But not in this case. This boy was gifted. Other children his age did things quickly, without thinking. Jumping Badger was different. He thought first, and then he acted.

In the past, Lakota children did not go to school. But they still had teachers. A boy's father chose his son's teacher. This was usually a brother or a **brother-in-law**. Returns Again asked his brother, Four Horns, to teach his son. Four Horns agreed. He taught the boy to ride. He taught him how to hunt. He showed him how to make a bow and arrows.

7

A Boy Called Slow

Slow lived with his uncle so that he could learn more from him every day. Four Horns (see box) was a wise man and a leader of his people. Slow developed into this type of person as well. Even as a young boy, Slow was already showing he had the four Lakota **virtues**: generosity, wisdom, bravery, and **fortitude**.

There was a contest among the boys to shoot the most beautiful bird. One boy shot at a bird. He missed. But his arrow got stuck high in a tree. The boy was upset. It was his best arrow. Slow aimed his arrow at the one stuck in the tree. His aim was true. He hit the arrow. Both arrows fell from the tree. But the other boy's arrow broke. He was very angry and blamed Slow for breaking his arrow. To avoid an argument, Slow gave the boy his own best arrow. Four Horns was impressed. His nephew was an excellent shot. He was kind and generous. And he was wise to avoid a fight over a broken arrow.

Four Horns

(about 1814–1887)

Four Horns was a respected Lakota leader. He was the one who persuaded other Lakota leaders to elect Sitting Bull as their one supreme chief when the United States Army threatened to destroy the Lakotas' way of life. Four Horns was Sitting Bull's loyal friend until he died in 1887.

This Oglala man is wearing a horned headdress and holding a bow, arrows, and a tomahawk.

First buffalo hunt

When Slow was about 10 years old, Four Horns took him on his first buffalo hunt. For the Lakota, hunting was not a sport for fun. They needed to hunt for food and other things their families needed to live. It took skill and bravery to become a good hunter. Hunting buffalo was dangerous. A man could be trampled to death if he fell off his horse. Despite his uncle's warnings, Slow rode boldly into the middle of the herd. He shot and killed a bull buffalo.

Four Horns was proud of his nephew's courage. But he was a little angry, too. It seemed reckless. Why go after a bull when there were cows that could be taken more safely and easily? Slow explained that the cow had a calf. If he shot the mother, what would happen to the calf? Slow then gave Four Horns yet another reason to be proud: He told his mother to give the best meat from his kill to a **widow** who had children to feed.

American bison (buffalo) are the largest land animal in North America.

Did you know?

The buffalo, or American bison, is a huge animal. Males can weigh more than 2,000 pounds (900 kilograms). They run as fast as 35 miles per hour (56 kilometers per hour). In the past, the Lakota depended on the buffalo for many things. They ate its meat. They used its **hide** to make clothing and **tipi** covers. Its horns and bones were made into tools. Its tail hairs decorated toys and clothing. Its teeth were strung onto necklaces. Every part had a use.

"Buffalo Bull Who Sits Down"

Around the same time Slow was hunting his first buffalo, Returns Again was with another hunting party. One night he and some other men were sitting around a campfire. A white buffalo bull appeared. It reared up, grunted, and stomped back down. It did this four times. Four is a **sacred** number to the Lakota.

Returns Again knew this was no ordinary buffalo bull. The others were afraid. Returns Again was the only one who understood that the grunts were words. He had the gift of communicating with the "four-leggeds." The bull had given Returns Again a gift of four names. The first was "Buffalo Bull Who Sits Down." Returns Again took this name for himself.

The Lakota drew pictures of important events to record their history. This painted hide (skin) shows them at war with the U.S. **Cavalry.**

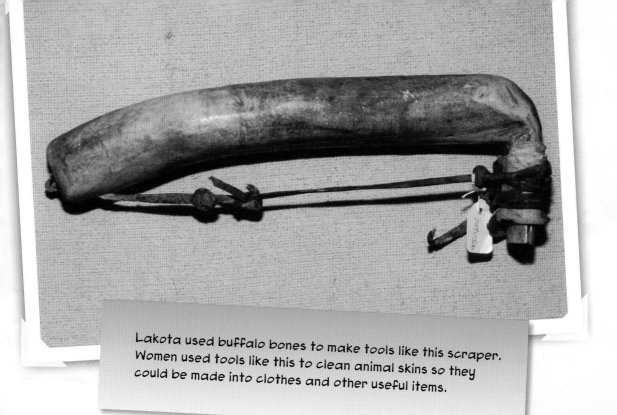

Lakota used buffalo bones to make tools like this scraper. Women used tools like this to clean animal skins so they could be made into clothes and other useful items.

Slow's first coup

Warriors showed their bravery when they met their enemy in battle. The bravest warriors counted **coup**. This was when a warrior rode up next to his enemy, hit him with a **coup stick**, and then rode away unharmed. When Slow was 14, he went on a raiding party. His father and Four Horns thought he was too young to fight, but they let him watch. Instead, the boy galloped toward the enemy. Slow slammed his coup stick down on a Crow warrior's arm, knocking him off his horse. It was his first coup.

Did you know?

Among the Lakota, white eagle feathers were earned for counting coup. Red feathers showed that a warrior had been wounded in battle. The U.S. military has a similar award for soldiers wounded in battle. It is called the Purple Heart.

A Warrior and a Sun Dancer

Buffalo Bull Who Sits Down honored his son with a single eagle feather that symbolized the **coup**. He also gave him a shield, a fine horse, and a new warrior name: Sitting Bull. The father took for himself the second name the White Buffalo had told him, and he was known as Jumping Bull from then on. His son became known as Sitting Bull. Young Sitting Bull had shown his generosity, bravery, and wisdom. Now he was going to prove he had the fourth Lakota **virtue**: **fortitude**.

Sun Dance

Around 1856 Sitting Bull danced the **Sun Dance** for the first time. The Sun Dancer prepares by fasting (not eating for a time) and cleansing in a **sweat lodge**. Then the **ritual** begins. His arms and chest are pierced many times with sharp bones or sticks that **skewer** the skin. Leather ropes tie the skewers to the trunk of a cottonwood tree in the center of a large circle. The Sun Dance circle is covered with sharp gravel to cut the dancer's feet. The Sun Dancer blows a whistle and stares into the sun.

The Sun Dance can last hours, or even days. Sometimes the Sun Dancer is hoisted up into the air. Other times he pulls until the skewers rip from his skin. Sun Dancers enter a **trance**. Sometimes they have visions, which help them make important decisions. The Sun Dance was the most important Lakota ritual. By becoming a Sun Dancer, Sitting Bull showed his deep commitment to his people and their traditional way of life.

This representation of a Sun Dance
was published in a magazine in 1875.

Strong Hearts

Sitting Bull was still only a teenager when he joined the Strong Hearts. Only the bravest Hunkpapa warriors were invited into this society. Sitting Bull became one of the two red sash bearers. These were the bravest of the brave. They wore a red sash into battle. The sash was staked to the ground to show that the warrior would fight to the end.

The Strong Hearts protected their people. They also provided for them. Sitting Bull was responsible for making sure his people had enough buffalo. But there were fewer buffalo each day. Sitting Bull soon discovered why. The buffalo were being killed by the *Wasichus* (see box on page 17).

Miners tended to be rough men who wanted to get rich. They did not care about what they did to the land, and they were often cruel to American Indians.

The Lakota knew there was "yellow metal" on their land, but they had no use for it, so it was not valuable to them.

Gold and greed

In the late 1840s, gold was discovered in California. In the 1850s, more gold was found in the Rocky Mountains. After that, *Wasichu* settlers streamed west to join the Gold Rush. Their path went right through the Lakota lands. Some Lakota raided wagon trains, taking horses, cattle, and guns. The U.S. government sent soldiers to protect the white settlers. Sitting Bull didn't know it yet, but trouble was on its way.

Did you know?

Wasichu is the word Lakotas used word for a white American. It means "non-Indian," but is often misinterpreted to mean "greedy person" or "person who takes the fat." The Lakota saw whites as selfish and wasteful. *Wasichus* would kill a buffalo and take only its **hide**, leaving the meat to rot.

Family Man

Lakota men could have more than one wife at a time if they could provide for such a large family. Sitting Bull married many times. He had many children, and his family gave him joy. But love for family can turn to sadness when someone dies.

In 1851 Sitting Bull married Light Hair. She died giving birth to Sitting Bull's first son. In 1859 Sitting Bull's father was killed when Crow Indians invaded their village. Sitting Bull took revenge on the Crow warrior who had killed his father. But he did not let his revenge rage out of control. He spared the lives of two Crow women who were captured. Later, the women were returned to their own people.

Jumping Bull
(about 1846–1890)

In 1857 the Strong Hearts came across an enemy camp. The family there was no match for the Hunkpapa warriors. The only one left alive was a boy. He was around 11 years old. Sitting Bull arrived after the killing was over. The boy pleaded for his life. "Big brother, save me," he cried. Sitting Bull was touched. His own young son had just died. He had no younger brothers of his own. He adopted the boy as his brother. He called him Stays Back because the boy chose to remain with him instead of returning to his own people. Later he took the name Jumping Bull after Sitting Bull's father died. Jumping Bull grew to be a brave warrior and remained a loyal friend to Sitting Bull as long as he lived.

Some of Sitting Bull's family posed in front of a **tipi**, around 1890.

Manifest Destiny

The United States government had plans for the western lands, and its plans did not include American Indians. The U.S. government and white settlers believed they had a God-given right to the land going all the way to the Pacific Ocean. This was called Manifest Destiny. It didn't matter that there were already people living there. U.S. troops were sent west to control the Lakota. The soldiers of the United States Army wore dark blue uniforms. For this reason, the Lakota called them Blue Coats.

Sitting Bull began fighting the Blue Coats in the early 1860s. He did not hate the *Wasichu*. He just wanted them to leave his people and their land alone. "The Indians here have no fight with the whites," he once said. "Why is it the whites come to fight with the Indians?"

The Lakota were great warriors. But the U.S. troops had newer and better weapons. In 1864 Sitting Bull and 5,000 to 6,000 Lakota warriors battled 2,500 Blue Coats at Killdeer Mountain. The Lakota outnumbered the U.S. soldiers. But their arrows and muskets were no match for rifles and cannons. The Lakota lost badly.

Fort Laramie Treaty

In 1868 many Plains Indian chiefs signed a **treaty** called the Fort Laramie Treaty with the U.S. government. This agreement said that the Plains Indians could continue to live on their land near the Powder River. In exchange, the Plains Indians had to **assimilate**. They had to become farmers. They had to wear *Wasichu* clothing. They had to send their children to school to learn *Wasichu* ways.

This illustration from the 1870s shows the symbol for Manifest Destiny floating over the land, leading more white settlers West.

Supreme Chief of the Great Sioux Nation

Sitting Bull never signed any **treaty**. He didn't trust the *Wasichus*. He had seen that the white men had broken treaties before, and he believed they would do so again. Sitting Bull was right. After gold was found in the Black Hills, in what is now South Dakota, miners poured in, hoping to get rich. The Black Hills were **sacred** to the Lakota. This was the last straw. The Lakota had to do something. But what?

Some Lakota were already living on **reservations**. Others, including the Hunkpapas, had refused to give up their way of life. But resisting was dangerous. The *Wasichus* were strong. The Lakota needed a new strategy, or they would be wiped out. In 1869 Four Horns called many chiefs together. He told them they must unite under one chief to be strong enough to fight the *Wasichus*. The other chiefs agreed. They chose Sitting Bull as their leader. They also elected Crazy Horse (see box) as his second in command.

The Black Hills, which the Lakota call *Paha Sapa*, have grassy meadows such as this one, where game was once plentiful.

The Crazy Horse Memorial in the Black Hills of South Dakota honors the Oglala war leader who fought General George A. Custer at the Battle of Little Bighorn.

Crazy Horse

(about 1842–1877)

Crazy Horse was from the Oglala **tribe** of Lakota. He was the greatest Lakota warrior of his time. Some of his tribe had followed Chief Red Cloud to live on a reservation. But, like Sitting Bull, Crazy Horse wanted to save his people's way of life. He did this by leading warriors into battle. He was a military genius and invented new ways of fighting. Even U.S. Army officers had to admit that his warriors were the best **cavalry** they had ever seen.

"Agency Indians"

Sitting Bull was beginning to realize the *Wasichus* would never leave his land. They wanted the gold in the Black Hills. The U.S. government didn't formally declare war on the Lakota, but it acted as though it had.

Other Lakota chiefs saw they could not beat the *Wasichus*. Their people would be killed. So they agreed to go live on reservations. Reservations were also called Agencies. And the American Indians who lived there were called Agency Indians. Agency Indians were totally dependent on the U.S. government for their food, clothes, and everything else they needed. The Hunkpapas did not respect Agency Indians. They continued to fight against the Blue Coats alongside Sitting Bull and Crazy Horse.

A brave move

In 1872 U.S. troops were protecting railroad workers on Lakota land. Some warriors were showing off by running the "daring line." They would ride their horses within range of the soldiers' bullets to show their bravery. Sitting Bull told them to stop. They could not beat the soldiers that way. But the braves did not want to stop. They hinted that Sitting Bull was too old to be a brave leader.

To show how wrong they were, Sitting Bull calmly walked out into a field within range of the soldiers' rifles. He invited other warriors to come and share a pipe with him. Only three joined him. Sitting Bull passed the pipe as bullets whizzed by. Then he cleaned out the pipe, stood up, and walked back to his people.

Agency Indians stand outside Chief Red Cloud's house on the Pine Ridge Reservation in South Dakota in 1890.

The Battle of Little Bighorn

In 1876 Sitting Bull sent messages to all the Lakota and their **allies**. He asked them to help defend their homeland. Meanwhile, Sitting Bull needed spiritual guidance. The time for the **Sun Dance** was approaching. He needed to know where it should be held. He went off on his own. Then he had a vision of a rocky place with a blue streak like a lightning bolt. A Cheyenne elder knew the place. It was Deer Medicine Rocks. That was where they would hold the Sun Dance.

Sitting Bull was a warrior. He was also a Sun Dancer. His adopted brother pierced Sitting Bull's arms and chest with more than a hundred **skewers**. Streaming with blood, Sitting Bull danced around the pole. He danced all night and into the next day.

Then he entered a **trance** and had a vision. He saw Blue Coats falling from the sky, upside down. A voice said, "I give you these because they have no ears." This meant they would not listen. But there was more. It was a warning: "Do not take their things. Leave them as they lay." Sitting Bull knew a great battle was coming. And he knew his people would win.

Did you know?

Sitting Bull bore many scars. A bullet in his foot left him with a limp. Another bullet hit him in the hip and came out his back. These scars, plus the scars from his Sun Dances, were like badges of honor to his people.

Sitting Bull knew the Battle of Little Big Horn was coming.

The Battle of the Rosebud

After the Sun Dance, the Lakota moved their camp to Rosebud Creek, where there was fresh grass for their horses. Scouts told them that the Blue Coats were marching in from three directions. Sitting Bull's plan was to fight only if the soldiers attacked. But the younger Lakota warriors were eager for battle. Finally, Crazy Horse led the charge.

Fact VS. Fiction

Myth: Crazy Horse commanded his warriors like a general commands his troops.

Fact: Lakota warriors did not have to follow orders. Soldiers followed orders because they were afraid of what would happen to them if they didn't. Lakota warriors fought by Crazy Horse's side out of respect, not fear.

This image shows Sittng Bull and Crazy Horse before the Battle of Little Bighorn.

The Blue Coats had better rifles. But the Lakota had confidence in Sitting Bull's vision. They drove the Blue Coats back to their camp. But this was not the battle Sitting Bull foretold. That was to come eight days later at a place the Lakota called Greasy Grass. It is also known as Little Bighorn.

George Armstrong Custer

(1839–1876)

George Armstrong Custer graduated at the bottom of his class at West Point Military Academy. He won fame as a Civil War hero. But other officers knew he took foolish risks. In the late 1860s, Custer went west to become an "Indian Fighter." The Lakota had nicknames for all the U.S. officers. They called Custer "Long Hair" because his blond, wavy locks hung down to his shoulders.

Little Bighorn

The Lakota moved to a fresh camp in a bend of the Little Bighorn River. They enjoyed themselves, singing, dancing, and socializing. They had no idea that "Long Hair" Custer was on his way.

Custer's Indian scouts found the Lakota camp. Custer rushed to attack. Lakota warriors grabbed their weapons and jumped onto their horses. Sitting Bull was going to join the warriors, but his elderly mother stopped him. She told him he had nothing more to prove. His Sun Dance wounds were still fresh. He should let the young warriors fight this battle. Sitting Bull respected his mother's advice. He helped the women, children, and elderly to safety.

Fact VS. Fiction

Myth: Sitting Bull lured Custer into a trap at Little Bighorn.

Fact: The Lakota didn't know Custer's army was on its way. They did not even know it was Custer who attacked them. He had cut his hair short and was wearing the same blue **cavalry** uniform other officers wore.

This illustration shows one representation of Custer's Last Stand.

The Battle of Little Bighorn lasted only "as long as it takes a hungry man to eat his dinner," according to the Lakota. Custer and his men lay dead. The Sun Dancer's vision had come true. But Sitting Bull did not celebrate the victory. His young son had been kicked in the head by a horse and died. He saw his people looting the battlefield. They did not heed the warning of his vision. Because of this, future generations of Lakota would suffer at the hands of the *Wasichus*.

From Grandmother's Land to Wild West Show

The Battle of Little Bighorn took place in 1876, and it also came to be known as Custer's Last Stand. That same year, Americans back east were celebrating 100 years of freedom from British rule. They did not know what was happening in the West. News traveled slowly.

It was only after Fourth of July festivities that they learned Custer, their golden war hero and Indian fighter, was dead. They thought the American Indians were monsters. And they felt their leader, Sitting Bull, was the worst of all. But the Lakota saw things differently. Their monsters wore blue coats.

The U.S. Army attacked peaceful villages. They burned homes and killed women and children. Without shelter, warm clothes, and stored food, many American Indians died in the freezing winter weather. The situation seemed hopeless. Even Crazy Horse surrendered.

Only Sitting Bull held out. He led a thousand Hunkpapas across the border into Canada. The Lakota called it "Grandmother's Land," because Canada was part of the British Empire ruled by the Queen of England.

Sitting Bull stayed in Canada for four hard years. Many of those who had come with him went back and surrendered. Some of his own family chose **reservation** life instead of staying with him in Canada. There was little to hunt. The winters were brutal. They were starving. In 1881 Sitting Bull led his remaining followers back to U.S. soil. Sitting Bull said, "I wish it to be remembered that I was the last man of my **tribe** to surrender my rifle."

Major James Morrow Walsh of the Canadian Mounted Police was firm but fair in his dealings with the Lakota who crossed the border into "Grandmother's Land." He and Sitting Bull respected each other and became good friends.

Another way of life

Sitting Bull had been chief of the Lakota Nation. Now he was an Agency Indian. "A warrior I have been, now it is all over," he said. "A hard time I have."

His life as a warrior was over, but Sitting Bull's legend grew. Articles about him appeared in newspapers. He gave interviews. Opinions changed. *Wasichus* began to see Sitting Bull as a hero, not a villain. He became one of the most famous men in the United States.

In 1885 Sitting Bull was allowed to leave the reservation to join Buffalo Bill's Wild West show. The show traveled around the United States for a few months. Sitting Bull saw many *Wasichu* cities. He learned a lot about the *Wasichu* world on this trip.

Buffalo Bill (see box) paid Sitting Bull to be in his show. Sitting Bull gave most of the money he made to beggar children. His **culture** valued children and took care of them. He did not understand why Americans let their children live as beggars.

Buffalo Bill did not use the word "show" in his posters. He wanted people back east to think they were seeing what really happened in the Wild West.

Sitting Bull posed wearing a long war bonnet for this photograph with Buffalo Bill. Each feather represents a war honor. But Sitting Bull usually wore only a single feather in his hair.

Buffalo Bill

(1846–1917)

"Buffalo Bill" Cody got his name hunting buffalo to feed railroad workers out west. Then he became a showman. Performers in Buffalo Bill's Wild West show raced horses, did shooting tricks, and acted out scenes from history. The show traveled all over the United States and Europe. Sitting Bull considered Buffalo Bill a good friend.

Death Comes for Sitting Bull

While Sitting Bull was on the road with Buffalo Bill, the U.S. government was planning a new landgrab. The U.S. government had cut the food **rations** for the American Indians. Thousands were starving on **reservations**. Sitting Bull still felt a strong responsibility to his people. Buffalo Bill asked him to go to Europe with the show. Sitting Bull refused. He had been away from his people long enough.

Some American Indians believed **Ghost Dance** shirts like this one from the late 1800s had special magic that made them bulletproof.

Fact VS. Fiction

Myth: Sitting Bull was the leader of the Ghost Dance religion.

Fact: Sitting Bull saw that the Ghost Dance gave his people hope in an otherwise hopeless time. But he himself did not believe in the new religion.

Meadowlarks are songbirds. Only the male sings. Their song sounds like someone playing a flute. Many people find this "bird music" beautiful.

A death foretold

Soon after he moved to Standing Rock Reservation, a meadowlark spoke to Sitting Bull. This was not the first time Sitting Bull received a message this way. But this message was different. It foretold his death: "Your own people, Lakotas will kill you." Sitting Bull knew that he would die at the hands of his own people.

Ghost Dance

Sitting Bull returned to the Standing Rock Reservation. The people there had found a new religion. It was called the Ghost Dance. They believed if they practiced the Ghost Dance, their suffering would end. But the Ghost Dance religion upset the agent in charge of the reservation. His name was James McLaughlin. McLaughlin wanted to control everything and everyone on the reservation. He and Sitting Bull never got along. They had no respect for each other. McLaughlin gave orders to arrest Sitting Bull.

The killing of Sitting Bull

Early on the morning of December 15, 1890, 43 "Metal Breasts" (American Indian policemen) came to arrest Sitting Bull. Sitting Bull was living in a cabin with his family. Some of the Strong Hearts acted as his bodyguards and stayed close. But even the bravest warriors could not stop what happened next. There was a struggle. Shots were fired. The American Indian policemen shot Sitting Bull in the chest and head, killing him.

Sitting Bull's son Crowfoot was also shot dead. So was his adopted little brother, Jumping Bull, along with five of Sitting Bull's bodyguards. Six Metal Breasts were also killed.

There was a big funeral for the dead Metal Breasts. Many people attended. Sitting Bull was buried, too. But there was little ceremony. His family and friends were not there to honor him. The families of the dead American Indian police blamed Sitting Bull's family for their loved ones' deaths. Fearing for their lives, Sitting Bull's family and friends fled Standing Rock Reservation. The bodies of Crowfoot, Jumping Bull, and the Strong Heart bodyguards were left where they lay for days. Eventually they were buried in a mass grave.

Sitting Bull's family

Sitting Bull's family was in more danger from their own people than from the U.S. government. The U.S. Army ended up protecting them from the Metal Breasts' families. Later, Sitting Bull's family ran away from Standing Rock Reservation. Eventually, they made their way to the Pine Ridge Reservation.

This photo of Crowfoot was taken after his father, Sitting Bull, surrendered in 1881.

Ernie LaPointe put his family's oral history on paper in his book about his great-grandfather, Sitting Bull.

Ernie LaPointe

(born 1948)

Sitting Bull's great-grandson is trying to set the record straight about his famous ancestor. Like Sitting Bull, Ernie LaPointe is a **Sun Dancer** and follows Lakota traditions. He produced DVDs and wrote a book based on stories his mother (Sitting Bull's granddaughter) and other relatives told him about his great-grandfather. His careful research challenges some of the accepted "facts" about Sitting Bull's life and death that appear in other books.

Wounded Knee

Many of the Ghost Dancers left Standing Rock Reservation, too. They joined the **band** of a Lakota chief called Big Foot (Spotted Elk). The U.S. government sent troops to arrest Big Foot. They found the band near Wounded Knee Creek. Big Foot was very sick. The Lakota did not try to resist. Soldiers went into the Lakota camp to take away their guns. But a shot was fired, probably by mistake. The soldiers panicked. They opened fire on the Lakota. At least 150 Lakota men, women, and children died. Many more were wounded and died later. This brutal **massacre** is considered the last battle between white soldiers and American Indians.

Sitting Bull's family moved his bones from the original gravesite at Fort Yates, North Dakota, to this burial site in Mobridge, South Dakota, in 1953.

Fact VS. Fiction

Freedom of religion was one of the basic rights granted to Americans. But not all Americans enjoyed this right. Until recently, it was illegal for American Indians to practice their religious ceremonies. Some of them continued to do so in secret, keeping these traditions alive until they were once again free to express themselves as they wished.

Timeline

1830s
Jumping Badger (Sitting Bull) is born.

1841
Jumping Badger, now called Slow, kills his first buffalo.

1845
Jumping Badger earns his first coup in battle and is renamed Sitting Bull.

1846
Sitting Bull gets his first red feather for a war injury.

1861
The American Civil War begins.

1859
Sitting Bull's father dies in battle.

1856
Sitting Bull is shot in the foot during a battle, leaving him with a lifelong limp.

1851
The Fort Laramie Treaty is signed. (Sitting Bull's band, the Hunkpapa, does not sign).

July 1864
Sitting Bull suffers a defeat in the Battle of Killdeer Mountain.

Nov. 1864
More than 200 Cheyenne are killed by U.S. troops in the Sand Creek Massacre.

1865
The American Civil War ends.

1866
Crazy Horse leads Oglala warriors to attack and kill 80 U.S. soldiers in the Fetterman Massacre.

1876
Custer and all 210 of his men are killed in the Battle of Little Bighorn.

1874
Gold is discovered in the Black Hills (Paha Sapa), the western third of the Great Sioux Reservation.

1869
Sitting Bull is elected high chief of the Lakota Sioux.

1868
The Fort Laramie Treaty establishes the Great Sioux Reservation.

1877
Crazy Horse surrenders (and is killed four months later). Sitting Bull goes to the "Grandmother's Land" (Canada).

1881
Sitting Bull returns to the United States and surrenders at Fort Buford.

1885
Sitting Bull joins Buffalo Bill's Wild West show and tours the U.S.

1890
Sitting Bull is killed by American Indian police under the command of the U.S. government. The Wounded Knee Massacre ends American Indian resistance.

1889
The Ghost Dance religious movement begins.

1887
The Dawes Severalty Act, which distributes land to American Indians, goes into effect. Sitting Bull returns to the reservation to try to stop this landgrab.

Family Tree

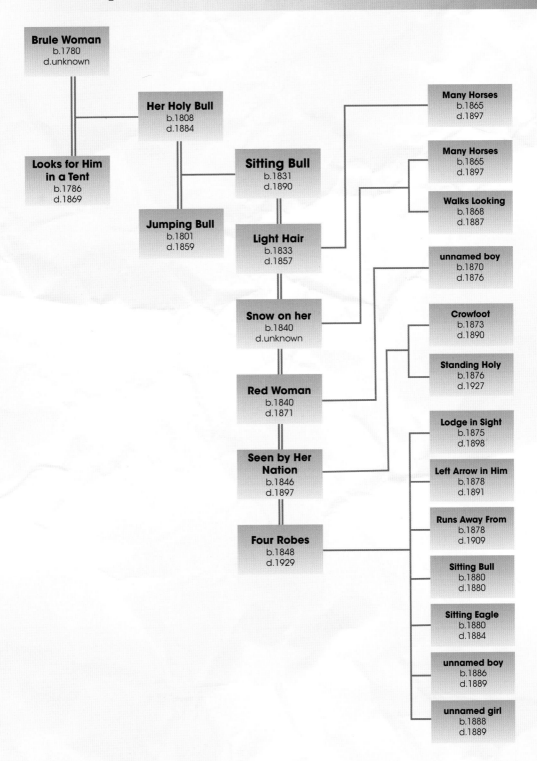

Brule Woman
b.1780
d.unknown

Her Holy Bull
b.1808
d.1884

Looks for Him in a Tent
b.1786
d.1869

Jumping Bull
b.1801
d.1859

Sitting Bull
b.1831
d.1890

Light Hair
b.1833
d.1857

Snow on her
b.1840
d.unknown

Red Woman
b.1840
d.1871

Seen by Her Nation
b.1846
d.1897

Four Robes
b.1848
d.1929

Many Horses
b.1865
d.1897

Many Horses
b.1865
d.1897

Walks Looking
b.1868
d.1887

unnamed boy
b.1870
d.1876

Crowfoot
b.1873
d.1890

Standing Holy
b.1876
d.1927

Lodge in Sight
b.1875
d.1898

Left Arrow in Him
b.1878
d.1891

Runs Away From
b.1878
d.1909

Sitting Bull
b.1880
d.1880

Sitting Eagle
b.1880
d.1884

unnamed boy
b.1886
d.1889

unnamed girl
b.1888
d.1889

Glossary

ally
group that agrees to help another group in a war

assimilate
to absorb one population or group into a different group's culture

band
group of American Indians who live together like an extended family

brother-in-law
brother of a person's husband or wife

cavalry
part of an army that fought on horseback

coup
French-Canadian term for signs of victory, counted by many American Indian tribes. There were usually three coups: one for killing an enemy, one for scalping, and one for being the first to strike an enemy.

coup stick
stick used by the Lakota to clobber an enemy—an honor higher than killing that enemy, as it showed greater bravery

cradleboard
wooden frame used by American Indian women for carrying an infant

culture
shared beliefs, traditions, and behaviors belonging to a certain group of people

fortitude
courage shown when under great pain or stress

Ghost Dance
American Indian religion of the late 1800s believed to restore traditional ways of life

hide
animal skin

massacre
brutal killing of many people at once

nomad
person who moves from place to place with no permanent home

ration
food allowance

reservation
land set aside by the government for a special purpose, such as a place for American Indians to live

ritual
religious ceremony in which people use symbols to express their cultural heritage

sacred
holy

skewer
make a hole through something with a pointed object

Sun Dance
American Indian religious ceremony

sweat lodge
special building used by American Indians to cleanse the body by sweating, using water poured over hot stones to create steam

tipi
cone-shaped shelter made of poles and animal hides

trance
state in which people behave as if they are asleep but are still able to understand what they experience around them

treaty
formal written agreement between two groups

tribe
group that shares a common purpose, language, and culture

virtue
behavior that is right or moral

widow
woman whose husband has died

Find Out More

Books

Collard, Sneed B., III. *Sitting Bull: Tatanka Iyotake*. New York: Benchmark, 2009.

Jeffrey, Gary, and Kate Petty. *Sitting Bull: The Life of a Lakota Sioux Chief*. New York: Rosen, 2005.

LaPointe, Ernie. *Sitting Bull: His Life and Legacy*. Layton, Utah: Gibbs Smith Publishers, 2009.

Stanley, George Edward. *Sitting Bull: Great Sioux Hero*. New York: Sterling Biographies, 2010.

DVDs

The Authorized Biography of Sitting Bull by his Great Grandson, by Ernie LaPointe. Produced by William Matson, ReelContact (www.reelcontact.com):
Part One: The Making of a Leader, 2007.
Part Two: Thank You Grandfather, We Still Live, 2008.

Biography: Sitting Bull: Chief of the Lakota Nation. A&E Home Video, 2005.

Sitting Bull: A Legacy. Timeless Media Group, 2008.

Websites

New Perspectives on the West
www.pbs.org/weta/thewest/people/s_z/sittingbull.htm
You'll find more information on Sitting Bull at this PBS website.

Sitting Bull Monument Foundation
www.sittingbullmonument.com/index.html
The Sitting Bull Monument Foundation protects Sitting Bull's gravesite and pays tribute to the great Lakota leader.

Smithsonian National Museum of the American Indian
www.nmai.si.edu/
You can find all kinds of information about the American Indians, including the Hunkpapa Lakota, as well as pictures of Sitting Bull.

Standing Rock Sioux Tribe
www.standingrock.org/
Here you can find information about the Standing Rock Sioux
Reservation and Tribe.

Places to visit

Crazy Horse Memorial
12151 Avenue of the Chiefs
Crazy Horse, SD 57730
605-673-4681
www.crazyhorsememorial.org/

**George Gustav Heye Center of the National Museum of the
American Indian**
Alexander Hamilton U.S. Custom House
One Bowling Green
New York, NY 10004
212-514-3700
www.nmai.si.edu/subpage.cfm?subpage=visitor&second=ny

Little Bighorn Battlefield National Monument
PO Box 39
Crow Agency, MT 59022
406-638-3217
www.nps.gov/libi/index.htm

Smithsonian National Museum of the American Indian
Fourth Street & Independence Avenue, SW
Washington, DC 20560
202-633-1000
www.nmai.si.edu/

Index